MADELAINE NUNN is an AWGIE winning writer, actor and producer working across theatre, film and radio since graduating from the VCA in 2015. Madelaine is the founder of Mad Nun Productions, co-founder of Three Birds Theatre, and Artistic Director of Rollercoaster Theatre. She has won The House of Oz Purse Prize, The Martin Lysicrates Prize, The Rebel Wilson Scholarship, The ATYP Foundation Commission and The Jopuka Eldersee Commission. She has been shortlisted for the Rodney Seaborn Playwrights Award three times; she is a three-time AWGIE nominee and has been longlisted for the Griffin Award and the Lysicrates Prize.

Notable writing credits include: *sitting, screaming* (The Old Fitz), *FLICK* (La Mama/Goodwood Theatre & studios), *SAAM* (ATYP), *Cactus* (La Mama/ RAV), *The Chapel, the Fire & the Dead Cat* (ATYP), *Summer at Suspended Stone Camp* (Jopuka Productions), *Kinder Surprise* (ABC RN) and *Bin Chicken* (ATYP/Griffin). With Three Birds Theatre, Madelaine is the co-writer and performer of *Garage Girls* (La Mama 2023), *Will This Show Take Off?* (Nati Frinj 2019), *Enter Ophelia* (La Mama 2018), *LadyCake* (Poppy Seed Theatre Festival 2016) and *Three Birds One Cock* (FRISK 2015; Adelaide Fringe 2016; Metanoia 2016; RAV Regional Tour 2016-19).

Madelaine has a number of acting credits, including: Flick in *FLICK* (Dir. Emily O'Brien-Brown), Alice in *Garage Girls* (Dir. Janice Muller), Mercutio in *Romeo and Juliet* for Essential Theatre (Dir. Alister Smith), Daisy in the feature film, *Two Heads Creek* (Dir. Jesse O'Brian), Xan in the Red Stitch production of *Desert 6:29pm* (Dir. Bridget Balodis), 2 in *The Three Graces* (Dir. Katie Cawthorne) and Maggie in *The Mill on the Floss* (Dir. Tanya Gerstle). You can keep up to date with Madelaine's work and her production company on Instagram @madonunnie and @madnunproductions.

Clare Hughes as Sam in New Ghosts Theatre Company's production of SITTING, SCREAMING *2024 at The Old Fitz Theatre. (Photo: Phil Erbacher)*

sitting, SCREAMING

Madelaine Nunn

CURRENCY PRESS
The performing arts publisher

CURRENCY PLAYS

First published in 2025
by Currency Press Pty Ltd,
Gadigal Land, Suite 310, 46–56 Kippax Street, Surry Hills, NSW 2010, Australia
enquiries@currency.com.au
www.currency.com.au

Typeset by Brighton Gray for Currency Press.
Cover shows Clare Hughes; photography by Phil Erbacher.
Cover design by Mathias Johansson for Currency Press.

Currency Press acknowledges the Traditional Owners of the Country on which we live and
work. We pay our respects to all Aboriginal and Torres Strait Islander Elders, past and
present.

Contents

***Disclaimer:** Please note the following introduction contains spoilers for* sitting, screaming. *If you have not yet seen or read the play, we recommend reading the introduction after finishing the script.*

Clare Hughes as Sam in New Ghosts Theatre Company's production of SITTING, SCREAMING *2024 at The Old Fitz Theatre. (Photo: Phil Erbacher)*

Introduction:
'Daring me to unsee': confronting difficult truths in *sitting, screaming*

'Louder together. Our voices are stronger in
numbers. Let's keep being brave.'

— Twitter, #LetHerSpeak Campaign

When Grace Tame addressed the National Press Club in 2021, one month
after she had been named Australian of the Year, she encouraged the
Australian public to sit in the discomfort of speaking about child abuse.
Madelaine Nunn's *sitting, screaming* leans into this sense of unease,
encouraging conversations about consent, resilience, institutional
failure, and peer support systems. These are not easy conversations to
have, but 'whilst they're disturbing to hear, the reality of what goes on
behind closed doors is more so,' said Tame in her Press Club speech.
sitting, screaming opens up these doors.

sitting, screaming is so much more than uneasy discussions, though.
It is funny. It embodies the brilliance and brevity of a young person on
the verge of adulthood. I didn't have the privilege of seeing Nunn's
work on stage, directed by Lucy Clements and starring Clare Hughes
at The Old Fitz—but Sam's character breathes and fizzes from every
inch of this script. Her voice is raw, authentic, sardonic, unfiltered,
dark, vulnerable, brave. Sam's life is teetering out of balance under
our very reading. It is clear from the outset that Nunn writes from the
experience of both a playwright and an actor. The script feels rhythmic,
and the action, although conservative in stage directions, jumps in
Sam's narrative retelling. The format notes alone are an investigation
into how to enliven written words on a page. Nunn understands raw
teenage emotions and captures the often chaotic inner voice of young
adulthood—evident across her other works such as *Cactus*, where
she has been credited for 'bring(ing) to life the awkwardness and
vulnerability of adolescence' (*Sydney Morning Herald*).

After my first read, I immediately began to imagine how my drama students could bring this script to life as a monologue. This text screams (and sits!) with performance potential for our young actors to demonstrate their range, particularly their ability to transform into different characters. It also presents a masterclass in the actor-audience relationship, with each aside from Sam imploring the audience to become her confidante. This text is ideal for our students who yearn to connect with a character they are familiar with: to explore the fast-paced transitions between comedy, pathos and rage through not just a young female voice but an *Australian* one, from a regional area, in what seems to be a public school. This setting is complete with a garish school uniform and the creatures that such an environment like a high school can breed: the teenage boys and their echoes of 'frigid' to describe girls who don't want to entertain their crudeness; the teachers, embarrassing in their humanity (the school counsellor's 'beetroot caught in the edge of her moustache hair'); the cliques; and conversations of composite female friendships.

We are being told this story through Sam's eyes, yet we are living it with her. When asked about her writing process, Nunn explained that, given the subject matter, 'it had to be one voice.' Sam is the main experience— she embodies the other voices—and works well to root the audience in the most crucial part of each scene. *sitting, screaming* occurs in the present with Sam's constant side-eye to the audience, voicing thoughts aloud that she often doesn't share with the other 'characters' on stage. She is stating, sharing, and living before us. We jangle along in the ride with her, moving between the counsellor's office, her lone friend Kaylah and her complicated homelife. We are taken with Sam when her crush on Mr David ignites—a teacher who has spoken kindly to her, who has seen her:

> And then I feel a tug.
>
> The moon.
>
> Glowing.
>
> […] But in that moment, it's like the moon feels me.
>
> And I tug back.

It's hard not to fall with her. It's not difficult to remember a time when someone you respected or looked up to took notice of you, when the rush of attention burned your face. The safe space that Sam seems to find with Mr David, though, soon feels alarmingly overfamiliar. He gently blurs lines. With her. With us.

And then, we are complicit in travelling with Sam through the experience of being groomed.

As Tame remarked in her speech, grooming is 'a concept that makes us wince and shudder and as such, we rarely hear about it. To the benefit of perpetrators. While it haunts us, and we avoid properly breaking it down, the complexity and secrecy of this criminal behaviour is what predators thrive on.'

Tame's address to the National Press emphasised that 'as a start, we should all be aware of what has been identified as the six phases of grooming.' Nunn deftly weaves these phases throughout *sitting, screaming,* mapping not only the experience of the victim but also the complicity and inaction of bystanders. If we are to educate our young people and the broader community, this text provides a pathway to understanding exactly how this can happen and where young people can easily fall through the cracks in our systems.

The Six Phases of Grooming

1. Targeting: identifying a vulnerable individual.

Sam is in under incredibly vulnerable circumstances that lend themselves to her manipulation. Her father is gravely ill with prostate cancer. She has been ostracised from her friendship group:

> I had more (*friends*) but then there was a coup and I was thrown out.
>
> Well, not *thrown out*, just stonewalled until I had the self-respect to step down from the friendship group.'

And perhaps the worst injustice: she's forced to meet with the school counsellor to talk about how she's coping with it all. To sum up her adolescent coping mechanisms: 'Freshly dyed bright-blue hair. It doesn't look great.'

Jasmin, Sam's erratic and volatile classmate, experiences a similar isolation that, we later learn, also makes her incredibly vulnerable to the same perpetrator:

Apparently, Jasmine's stepfather used to burn cigarettes into her arms.

That's why she's covered in these little circle scars.

2. Gaining trust: establishing a friendship and falsely lulling the individual into a sense of security, by empathising and assuring safety

Mr David's consistent approach to Sam first establishes him as someone she can trust. It is gradual, subtle, precalculated: ' *"I'll leave the door open."'* We gain an insight into the way trust is established, abused and taken advantage of.

He is first her ally. He doesn't acknowledge the beer in Sam's hand at the fish and chip shop:

> He clocks the beer.
>
> […] *'Have a good night.'*
>
> He winks at me.
>
> Then waves goodbye.

He then becomes her 'saviour'. When Sam has no money at the canteen, he steps in to spot her financially:

> *'If there's an issue, just put it on my account.*
>
> […] *No-one should miss out on lunch.'*

He 'rescues' Sam during her panic attack:

> *'Nothing is wrong.'*
>
> […] *You are here.'*
>
> […] *You are safe.'*

He shows empathy for her by arranging a 'special considerations form' and shows he trusts her by confiding in Sam about other teachers: ' *"They're socially fucked up, and no-one knows how to wash out a coffee cup."'* He establishes a deeper connection, sharing aspects of his personal life:

> He tells me how unhappy he is at home.
>
> His wife's a lot of work.

He ultimately gains her trust: 'We've become … friends?'

3. Filling a need: playing the person who fills the gap in the individual's emotional support system

Mr David takes on the role of sympathiser while Sam is failing in her academic and personal life. His office becomes normalised as a refuge away from the classroom; 'it became a habit' for her to go to his office and hang out.

In a time when her family is distracted by her father's illness, Mr David presents himself as a witness for Sam's pain, which seems neglected by everyone else: ' *"I just want to say, I know it's not easy. Watching someone you love go through something like that that it's … lonely."*'

In a time where she feels inferior to her brother, and mainly unseen in the wake of his apparent successes as 'the fucking golden child', Mr David exploits Sam's feelings of invisibility and inadequacy. By offering the validation and attention Sam isn't receiving elsewhere, Mr David deepens her dependence on him.

4. Isolating: driving wedges between the target and their genuine supporters

Mr David belittles Sam's existing support networks, namely her best friend Kaylah and Miss Credlin, the school counsellor. He creates a wedge, establishing an 'us' and 'them':

> there are some people, like Kaylah and Miss Credlin who
> go through life with no problems.
> Those people can never understand.

Miss Credlin, as contemptible as Sam makes her out to be, is a support system who holds Sam accountable to working towards her own betterment: ' *"Vulnerability isn't a weakness. Telling people how you feel isn't a weakness. It's hard. […] I'll see you next week."*' Mr David undermines a professional who is in a position to expose his predatory nature. He purposefully condescends in his remarks about Miss Credlin, describing her as:

'a bit of a wet blanket sometimes.'

[…] 'Don't get me wrong, she's lovely but her position doesn't pay very well. So, we get whoever applies, unfortunately.'

5. Sexualising: exposing the target to sexual content to normalise it

Here, it is a quick descent. As an audience, we are in freefall in Scene 14. What began as emotional support tips into explicitly predatory behaviour. The previously blurred lines between concern and control suddenly become a stark abuse of power.

He likes my blue hair.

I remind him of a flower.

[…] 'Have you ever had one (a boyfriend)*?'*

*[…] **A small beat. A change in her.***

[…] 'So, you're not gay?'

[…] 'Do you think you're pretty?'

'You're the kind of girl I'd want my son to date. […] The type of girl I would have dreamed of dating in high school.'

[…] His lips touch mine.

They're wet.

This scene is devastating in its quietness. The audience, witnessing each calculated step, is placed in the uncomfortable position of realising how quickly and subtly this exploitation can unfold.

6. Maintaining control: striking a balance between causing pain and providing relief from that pain.

Abusers create confusion to scare their victim into silent submission. The intention is conditioning the target to feel guilt at the thought of exposing a person who also appears to care for them.

Sam is obviously affected by the abuse, immediately recognising that she's at risk:

I hate him.

I avoid him for as long as I can but he catches me off guard.'

Mr David, however, twists the situation by shifting the blame onto Sam, framing her as the instigator who needs to apologise for her actions:

'You don't have to do it now; you can take your time if you want.

[…] I know you didn't mean it. It's just a crush.'

Sam is backed into a corner:

I smile.

And say—thank you.

Because what else am I going to do?

Despite wanting to tell Miss Credlin, Mr David maintains control over the situation by intervening in Sam's one-on-one with the counsellor.

When Sam begins to build courage to speak, it vanishes under his presence:

Ready to unleash

To fight back.

When I hear it

His voice.

Getting louder and louder.

I try to hold on

But the courage.

It's gone.

This phase of grooming, manipulation of guilt, indebtedness and fear is precisely what makes speaking out so difficult. This is why understanding these patterns of behaviour is critical.

Hauntingly, there is a gap in the action between Scene Seventeen and Eighteen. We are left to consider what has been left unsaid. When Tame won her Australian of the Year Award in 2021, she recalled,

'I remember him saying, 'Don't make a sound.' Well, hear me now.'

Nunn navigates the courage it takes for Sam to speak the truth and empowers us, as an audience, to consider her situation with empathy rather than judgment. We sit with her in the struggle of speaking up and speaking out. The play's uncapitalised title hangs over the space like an unfinished thought—suspended in the present participle, the 'doing' ongoing and indefinite. The action of this text must unfold in the present tense, reminding us that hindsight often raises questions like, 'why didn't you just …?' The truth of the moment is that it is hard. As we have joined Sam in each scenario, we are better placed to understand the complexity behind the choices that others make.

We finally acknowledge the rat. In Scene Four, Sam sees and pretends to unsee a 'big, black-eyed mutant rat' running loose in the fish and chip shop—a foreshadowing of what she will later confront, which is the uncomfortable truth:

> Horror-movie shit.
>
> But we just had to pretend like we didn't see it.
>
> Because if you acknowledge that you saw the rat. Then the food tastes bad. And then you can't go there anymore. And then your life is ruined.

The rat represents something rotten that everyone sees, but no one dares to talk about. Ignoring it preserves the illusion of normalcy. Acknowledging it would demand change. However, the second sighting marks Sam's tipping point; she can no longer 'unsee' what's happening to her and Jasmin. She chooses truth over denial.

> The rat.
>
> Daring me to look away.
>
> Daring me to unsee it.
>
> But I see it.
>
> I can't unsee it.
>
> It's fucking disgusting.

We are offered the opportunity to discuss how silence is not neutral, and how metaphor can give voice to what feels unspeakable. Choosing not to speak, like pretending not to see the rat, allows harm to continue. Jasmin does join Sam in speaking out, a gesture echoed by countless untold stories of abuse.

In her interview with Eastside Radio FM, Nunn observes, 'when tackling a complex topic, it's important to have hope at the end. There is hope.' When the play ends, and Sam has found the courage to speak, she is hopeful. Her story echoes the solidarity and staunchness of the #LetHerSpeak campaign, co-established by Tame and journalist and sexual assault survivor Nina Funnell.

sitting, screaming is a text we can use not only as a powerhouse model of the craft of acting, but also as an educational tool. When addressing the Press Club, Tame described grooming is 'unfortunately too common in occurrence for us to hope that kids know this [is a serious topic] … I challenge our education system to look for ways to more formally educate our children. Because we know that education is our primary means of prevention.' Unpacking a harrowing experience of abuse through empathising with a young central character like Sam helps highlight real-world nuance, more than any PowerPoint presentation or siloed health lesson. It personifies the power of drama.

This text is more than a performance. It's a conversation in solidarity with voices like Tame's. It is an aid for educating the next generation in empathy, awareness, and advocacy.

Ellen Osborne
Drama and English teacher, NSW

Writer's Note

Once the play has been written, it's sometimes hard to know when and how it began ... It can feel like a hazy one-night stand or some immaculate conception. This is not the case with *sitting, screaming*.

Lucy and I first met on a blind theatre date at an RSL in Redfern in 2019. We both ordered a watered-down gin and tonic and sat on high black stools in a carpeted, upstairs room, next to the pokies. This is exactly where theatre is made. Ha! Venue aside, we were both excited to meet and recognised that our careers and efforts were paralleling each other in both Sydney and Melbourne. We were both ambitious theatre-makers trying to see more female-driven stories with complex female characters on stage.

And so, it began. One day on Zoom, we did a theatre focus group to a bunch of female actors. I pitched around a few ideas and then I came to this one. Suddenly everyone was talking—Zoom etiquette was out the window. Stories started pouring, memories were triggered, it was 'yes, and' all around. The generation didn't matter. There was a deep universality to the experience of being a young woman in high school. We all understood the brutality, the vulnerability, the camaraderie and the isolation.

sitting, screaming is inspired by the resilience of young women. Their strength, their complexity, their humour, the way they see and experience the world. I wanted to give the platform to a young, complicated character and go on her journey, giving her the narrative power to tell her story. I didn't set out to write a solo show, but it became increasingly evident through the creative process that this story had to have one voice. The only voice that mattered.

The core question for me was, how do we keep letting our most vulnerable people fall through the cracks? What is it that we miss? What are we overlooking? What are the assumptions or unconscious bias that predators rely on?

Theatre has the potential to challenge preconceived ideas and give insight into experiences outside of our own. In a time where it's so easy to dehumanise each other, theatre has the power to show deep humanity, empathy and compassion for other people. As a theatre-maker, it's integral that all my work has humour and levity, even when exploring dark and complex themes.

This is a tough play but it's also a funny play. It's candid and it's raw. Most importantly, it's hopeful. We must leave the theatre with hope, with the idea that we can change the world or our behaviour, even in the smallest way.

Political theatre is theatre that touches the heart as well as the head—ideas and feelings should stand side by side. Speak up, ask questions! Connect with each other. There is plenty of change to be made!

Acknowledgements

Thank you so much to Lucy Clements, Emma Wright, Clare Hughes, New Ghosts Theatre Company, The Old Fitz, Anthony McGirr (my love and unofficial dramaturg), Maureen Nunn, Colin Nunn, Helen Donnard, The S,B&W Foundation, Aarne Neeme, Luna Ng, Hailley Hunt, Sam Cheng, Natalie Baghoumian, Jade Julian, Helena Cielak, Madeline Li, Pip Rath. Thank you to everyone who came and supported this new Australian work!

Clare Hughes as Sam in New Ghosts Theatre Company's production of SITTING, SCREAMING *2024 at The Old Fitz Theatre. (Photo: Phil Erbacher)*

sitting, screaming was first produced by New Ghosts Theatre Company at The Old Fitz Theatre, Sydney, Gadigal Country, on the 20 September 2024, with the following cast:

SAM   Clare Hughes

Director, Lucy Clements
Producer, Emma Wright
Production Manager, Amy Norton
Lighting Designer, Luna Ng
Set & Costume Designer, Hailley Hunt
Composer & Sound Designer, Sam Cheng
Stage Manager, Natalie Baghoumian
Lighting Design Mentor, Veronique Benett
Assistant Director & Understudy, Jade Julian
Assistant Producer, Helena Cielak
Assistant Sound Designer, Natesha Ham

Clare Hughes as Sam in New Ghosts Theatre Company's production of SITTING, SCREAMING *2024 at The Old Fitz Theatre. (Photo: Phil Erbacher)*

CHARACTERS

SAM. Almost eighteen. Freshly dyed bright-blue hair. It doesn't look great.

NOTES ON THE TEXT

The character of SAM embodies all voices.

The play moves at fairly fast clip.

Moving between place and time.

Words in (brackets) are unspoken.

Whole sentences in *italics* indicate SAM's dialogue.

Partial words in *italics* indicate stress.

Whole sentences in *italics* and quotation marks represent another person speaking.

Words in ***bold italics*** are stage directions.

— is a cut-off.

I strongly encourage the producer to collaborate with artists from diverse backgrounds in the casting and presentation of this work.

There comes a point in a teenage girl's life when you realise everything you've ever known was a lie and you have to rebuild yourself from the ground up.

Clare Hughes as Sam in New Ghosts Theatre Company's production of SITTING, SCREAMING *2024 at The Old Fitz Theatre. (Photo: Phil Erbacher)*

SCENE ONE

School Counsellor's office. SAM sits.

I count six.

Empty teacups.

All of them coated in a film of white skin.

One of them says,

Live, Love, Laugh ellipsis … *a lot.*

Another says,

Keep Calm, Carry On.

It's embarrassing.

The clichés almost undermining her position.

But at this point, I think she should go all out; put on fountain noises and turn the diffuser up to a hundred.

Ride that essential-oil high.

Although, cracks are showing.

The tiny rake in the miniature Zen Garden is broken.

Splintered apart where the shaft meets the handle.

It was probably her. She probably did it. Alone. One lonely Friday night. Furiously raking. Until it snapped.

So, instead I just finger the sand.

Dunno why?

Some primal urge to push my finger into something soft.

Plus, I need to do *SOMETHING* while I wait for her to finish *deep throating her panini.*

Miss Credlin clears her throat.

'New hair?' she says,

Food rolling around her mouth.

'Blue? … That's a statement—like a rockstar.'

Then wipes the front of her teeth with her tongue.

'Did you do it yourself?'

RUDE.

A very expensive hairdresser did it, actually.

If you count some chick in a garage exchanging haircuts for old iPhones.

'Well, it looks good.'

It doesn't.

'I've got to do something with my hair, not highlights, I've thought about it but it's too dry for highlights. I guess I should probably drink more water. Ha! The answer is, always drink more water!'

Put that on a coffee cup.

'Sorry?'

Nothing.

She quickly has a sip of her plastic drink bottle and takes one more not-so-secretive bite of her panini.

Gobbling it down like a bird on heat

Before turning to ask—

'How are you coping with it all?'

Do you think it's in the job description?

To have that voice.

That voice she has.

That they all have.

Dropping into a lower register, almost a whisper.

Like there's a baby or a gunman asleep in the corner of the room and we've got to be very quiet, so they don't wake up crying and shoot us in the face.

'How are your stress levels?'

There's a bit of beetroot caught in the edge of her moustache hair.

'You look tired.'

Dangling tauntingly in the corner.

'Have you been getting enough sleep?'

Clinging for dear life.

'SAM!'

Huh?

'Have you been getting enough sleep?'

SO much sleep.

'And the breathing exercises? Are you doing them?'

SO much breathing.

'So, they're working then?'

I nod.

She nods.

'Good.'

She starts to write when the beetroot *flings* itself off.

Onto my sheet.

'Oops!'

She tries grabbing at it with her fingers. But it just slides around, trailing a purple stain.

The opposable thumb is wasted on her.

Finally, she scoops it up with her nail and *pops* the beetroot into her mouth.

Grotty.

She's made the form grotty.

'Sorry about that ... where were we ... ?'

She looks up through her glasses at the clock.

And that's time!

So, can I go now or what?

She looks at me, tilting her head to the side.

Like a cat on anti-depressants.

'If you're not in the mood to talk then, yes, you're free to leave.'

Yeah, it's my *mood* preventing us from connecting.

I open the door, Jasmin's waiting in the corridor.

And then Miss Credlin stops me with a hand on my shoulder.

'Vulnerability isn't a weakness. Telling people how you feel isn't a weakness. It's hard. But it isn't a weakness. I'll see you next week.'

I roll my eyes at her—making sure she sees.

SCENE TWO

The Oval.

I find Kaylah sitting on a bench highlighting her notes. Hunched over like a dinosaur.

Cramming.

She has blue pen all over her face. Her hair is oily as fuck.

She doesn't look up, even when I stand in front of her.

Blocking the sun.

She's angry 'cos I forced her to smoke weed with me last week.

She got so anxious she vommed all over her computer, now her escape key doesn't work.

You can't seriously still be mad at me.

'I'm not mad, I'm focused.'

Can you not be focused for a second?

'No. I've lost many vital brain cells at the worst possible time.'

You'll grow them back.

'Brains don't fully mature until you're twenty-five, you know that!'

How much more maturing can we do between now and twenty-five?

'Do you own an umbrella?'

What?

'Do. You. Own an umbrella?'

No?

'Then, you've got a LONG way to go until adulthood. I should've trusted Harold.'

She's still traumatised by the hand puppet giraffe that came to our school when we were kids.

The one that was obviously totally cooked itself but still had the gall to tell us not to do drugs.

Hypocrite Harold.

Those highlighters are probably fucking with her brain more than a puff of weed would've.

Having one friend is not ideal.

I had more but then there was a coup, and I was thrown out.

Well, not *thrown out*, just stonewalled until I had the self-respect to step down from the friendship group.

Someone thought I was flirting with a boyfriend. It's always petty.

It's okay, though.

They were kind of shit friends in the end.

Not like Kaylah.

You always know where you stand with Kaylah. She's a forever friend.

Plus, she lives three streets away, we've carpooled since we were four. Her mum's the kind of mum to always have mints in the glovebox.

Explains a lot about her personality.

I try one last attempt at salvation.

SAM *drops to her knees.*

I'm sorry. Please forgive me. I'll do anything!

She slams her book shut in a huff.

'Come with me to assembly and I'll think about it.'

Thank you! But can we stand near the back?

SCENE THREE

Assembly.

A ringing over the loudspeaker.

'Possibility and promise.'

Mrs Bourke splutters into the microphone.

The p's blasting our eardrums.

'You are staring down the rest of your lives, YOU are in the driver's seat, we are merely your stewards, journeying to a better future.'

I slow clap.

Kaylah glares.

Then Mr David takes the stand.

Everyone collectively quietens down.

A first name for a last name is real BDE.

Big Dick Energy.

Get nothing from her.

You gotta admit, the suit and tie's a bit much. He knows this is a public school, right?

'What you wear reflects who you are,' Kaylah hisses.

Regurgitating a quote, no doubt.

And yet they make us wear a lemon-yellow blouse?

What's that meant to reflect?

She death-stares me to be quiet.

She loves Mr David.

Everyone loves Mr David.

Especially because he's a feminist.

After Daniel FitzGibbon was caught hiding in the girls' toilets filming Lily C. changing a tampon, Mr David sat all the boys down.

Did a 'respect for women' session every Tuesday for a month. Forced them all to go, otherwise he'd cancel sport.

Daniel FitzGibbon apologised to every single one of us.

Real tail-between-the-legs moment.

And then all the boys donated ten dollars to the Breast Cancer Foundation.

Which I thought was weird but it's the *gesture that counts.*

Although less than half an hour after the last session, Liam yells at the girls:

'Wet T-shirt competition!'

Puts his finger over the bubbler and blasts us with water.

We all groan.

And turn away.

Our lemon-yellow shirts, now see-through.

'Fucken frigid!'

I guess that's all it was.

A gesture.

SCENE FOUR

Home.

I get home.

The sink's filled with dishes.

Technically, that's my job but CBF doing them right now.

The house is quiet.

Dad must be asleep upstairs.

Joe's not in his room, must be out—so that's a win.

Mum's written a note.

Dinner's in the …

She hasn't even finished the sentence.

I open the fridge.

There's beer, a bag of bendy carrots, off yogurt and some probiotic tablets in the door.

Not exactly sure what Mum had in mind.

I look around. The place is a dump.

None of the jobs are done.

I think about doing them … but fuck it.

Instead, I take a beer and walk to the fish and chip shop down the road.

It wasn't always like this.

Dad was an accountant.

Still is.

Then he got sick.

Prostate cancer.

'Too much wanking!' Mum used to joke without a smile.

I didn't even know he had cancer until I read the card on some flowers that arrived at our doorstep.

It was their weird way of trying to protect me.

Whatever.

I mean, I had wondered why my dad had turned into a small grey sultana that never left our couch.

It's not true.

About the cancer.

Has nothing to do with wanking.

Imagine if it did … we'd all be in trouble.

It's genetic, or random. Or both.

It's bad timing, Mum was just about to quit her job.

I think most of life is bad timing.

A little bit of life is good timing.

So now she has to do extra shifts at the job she hates. Which is why she's never home.

Plus, Dad's developed a *smell*.

Somewhere between cream cheese and the inside of a suitcase.

I guess that's what happens when you sit in the *same spot* wearing the *same trackies* for a month.

The chip shop's always busy.

I feel bad for the lady that works there. She looks … sticky.

I wonder if she ever thinks about plunging her hand into the deep fryer.

Just to know how it felt.

Once Kaylah and I saw a rat scurry out from behind the counter and dart under the drink fridge.

I'm not talking a small baby rat, one that you could confuse with a native mouse or something.

I'm talking a big, black-eyed mutant rat.

Horror-movie shit.

But we just had to pretend like we didn't see it.

Because if you acknowledge that you saw the rat. Then the food tastes bad. And then you can't go there anymore. And then your life is ruined.

So, we erase that memory.

What memory?

Shrugs.

Exactly.

I'm waiting for my order when I bump into him.

I don't recognise him at first.

Without the suit and tie.

'Sarah?'

Fuck.

I quickly hide my beer behind my back.

Fuck.

It's so obvious. Why did I bring it?! I don't even really like the taste. I just like the feeling.

Er, Sam. But. Close.

'Ah, Sam. That's right. Don't hold it against me, Sam. I'm off duty.'

He puts his hands in the air like he's a criminal surrendering.

Like getting my name wrong is a crime.

Laughs awkwardly.

'I didn't know this was your local?'

What?

'Fish and chip shop?'

Oh. Yeah. I live down the road.

Drips from the can run down my leg.

'Are you here by yourself or?'

Yep. I mean, no! I'm meeting some friends. Later.

He raises his eyebrows like he doesn't believe me.

*[**Yelled**] 'One battered fish, small chips, two scallops and extra sauce?'*

Extra sauce, that's me.

Saved by the chip lady.

I collect my dinner and hold it in my arms like a hot paper baby.

Well, see ya—

I go to leave.

He clocks the beer.

'Hey Sam.'

Fuck.

Here it comes.

Detention. Call to Mum. Fucking exactly what I need.

Yep?

Small pause.

'Have a good night.'

He winks at me.

Then waves goodbye.

I'm so stunned I walk in the opposite direction.

Turns out I was wrong.

He might not be so uptight after all.

SCENE FIVE

Basketball courts.

It's not even ten a.m.

A crowd of people are gathered in a circle on the basketball courts.

There must be a fight!

I join in—poking my head between shoulders.

Get out my phone, like everyone else.

Content is content.

It's not a fight.

Just Jasmin.

Smashing a laptop. A *school* laptop.

Hashtag brave.

She's really going for it.

Slamming it on the ground.

Over and over and over again.

It's mesmerising.

The glass ricochets around her like glitter.

Like a witch conjuring a spell.

Her anger.

It's in her mouth.

In her hands.

In her shoulders.

And for a heartbeat, it's in me too.

I've never been in a brawl before, but in this moment if someone even dared look at me the wrong way, I feel like I could gouge out their eyes and bite off their ears.

Apparently, Jasmin's stepfather used to burn cigarettes into her arms.

That's why she's covered in these little circle scars.

She says it was just from chicken pox.

Either way, I've always felt bad for her.

[*Amused*] Mrs Lorry is choking on her whistle, she's blowing it so hard.

A whistle is not going to stop a tornado!

Then Mr David comes in.

Scoops her up into his arms.

She spits at him.

'Oooooh!'

The crowd cries.

Feels medieval.

And yet,

Totally modern.

Her arms and legs flail, like a rag doll, possessed.

It's ramping up

About to get heated

And then

It's extinguished.

She's run out of breath?

Admitted defeat.

The bell rings.

And the spectacle's over.

SCENE SIX

School Canteen.

'Hurry the fuck up!'

Someone yells at me down the line.

I'm stuck at the counter.

For some reason my card's declining.

I mean … I know the reason.

I have no money.

But I skipped breakfast and now I'm starving.

Who the fuck charges five dollars for a fucking offal meat pie anyway?

'Alright love, what are we going to do?'

Hair-net-lady asks.

Fuck.

This is embarrassing.

'Is there a friend nearby that could help you out?'

I look around.

Liam stares back.

'Nice hair. What are you cosplaying as? A swimming pool?'

I want to fucking stab him in the throat with a ballpoint pen.

… It's fine. Don't worry about it.

'Is everything okay?'

He turns up beside me.

Bending down to look through the window.

Yep. All good.

In this moment, if you said he was the tallest man in the world, I'd believe you.

'If there's an issue, just put it on my account.'

No, no, there's no issue. I just realised I'm not actually hungry.

He holds me in his eyes. Sweat patches under his arms.

'No-one should miss out on lunch.'

He says, like it's a teacher's creed.

Which I think is cringe.

But I am hungry, and he is offering so …

One meat pie, a can of coke and—

[**Mr David**] *'Extra sauce?'*

He finishes my sentence.

… Ah yeah, only if it's okay?

He laughs, patting me on the back.

'Get whatever you want.'

Then walks away.

So, I do.

I add a KitKat and a packet of chips to my order.

Stuff them in my pocket for later.

SCENE SEVEN

Hospital.

Dad's always hated noise.

So, the hospital beeping must be driving him insane. He'd never complain.

He's stoic like that.

I sit on an oversized plastic chair

Laptop balanced between my legs.

Doomscrolling.

He's here because he collapsed waiting for the kettle to boil.

Well, that's what I *think* happened. No-one *tells* me anything.

I dropped him some books. Mum couldn't stay.

Joe's 'busy' studying, apparently.

Dad's in bed, watching a kid get covered in green goo on the mini TV hanging from the ceiling.

You'd think they'd have iPads by now.

Maybe they do.

Maybe this is just a really shit hospital.

He reaches towards me. Waves his hand, limply in my direction.

[*Low energy*] *'What's this crap I'm watching?'*

His lips are dry. Crusty on the outside.

It's an American game show where you answer questions and if you get them wrong, you get slimed.

'Slimed?'

Yeah.

'What kind of questions?'

Pop culture questions.

'Oh.'

I don't think you're the target audience.

He makes a gruff sound.

'Turn it off, would ya? Talk to me.'

He's got silver stubble. Hasn't been clean-shaven in a while.

I pick a hair off his face.

'Don't mind them, they're just me sparklies.'

I twist the hair in my fingers.

'Go on then, tell me what you're working on.'

Ah, just doing some maths homework.

'Maths? Good to hear. I was worried that ... ahh ... That this might be a bit ... you know ... for you.'

He looks exhausted.

His bags are so big I feel like I could curl up and lie under his eyes.

'And you're still keeping up with the others?'

Yeah, of course. Last week I topped my class in an English essay about history and representation.

I lie.

'That's my girl.'

He flashes me his teeth, first real smile in months.

'I'm so proud of you, kiddo. You haven't let all this distract you.'

SAM *starts to drift away.*

'You've made your old man proud.'

Yeah ...

Her world falls away at the edges.

SAM *starts to breathe deeply.*

SCENE EIGHT

School.

SAM *is having a panic attack.*
She tries to control it.
She clutches at her chest, struggling to breathe.
She searches for a way out.

Fuck.

Can't

Fuck.

Breathe.

Slowly making her way to the ground.

Fuuuuuuuuck.

My chest

[***Gasping/struggling***] I don't want to die near the sports shed.

No!

Not real.

Just my

brain.

Lizard

brain

z, y, x,

z, y, x

The fuck comes after x?

Grass!

I'm on grass.

Birds.

Chirping.

The wind—on my skin.

Shoes.

Brown shoes.

A voice

Shadows.

His shadow.

His hand.

Lifts me

Off the ground.

My hands

Wet.

'Say it.'

Huh?

'Nothing's wrong.'

SAM *is confused.*

'Say it.'

Nothing's wrong … ?

'You are here. Say it.'

I am here?

'You are safe.'

She breathes out.

I am safe.

Calming herself down.

I am safe.

His office.

His desk is neat.

Serial-killer neat.

'I'll leave the door open.'

He tells me.

He must be super smart.

Framed certificates of his name line the wall behind his desk.

The way they do when you go to the doctor's.

One of those teachers who didn't *have* to be a teacher.

But took the profession for the greater good.

Thanks for before, but I'm actually totally fine now.

'It's very normal and I'm happy to help.'

He says, as he sits down.

He smiles.

Taking me in.

And then I see it.

On his desk.

A sheet

With a beetroot stain.

'Don't worry. It's just a chat. I've talked to Miss Credlin and this can be counted as one of your sessions.'

Of course they gossip about us in the staff room.

'Has she helped? Miss Credlin?'

Ah, yep, yeah. Very helpful.

He sniggers.

'Sam. You don't need to lie; you can be honest with me.'

His dark eyelashes curl around his eyes.

'I know she can be a bit of a wet blanket sometimes.'

Wow. Savage.

'Don't get me wrong, she's lovely but her position doesn't pay very well. So, we get whoever applies, unfortunately.'

That's comforting.

'Not to worry. She's not the only one looking out for our students' wellbeing. Now, correct me if I'm wrong; you're Joe's little sister.'

His legacy lives on. I'm surprised they haven't named a wing after him.

'You have the same eyes.'

Everyone says that.

'Better nose.'

Huh! Suck shit Joe.

'And you're friends with Kaylah Matherson, right?'

Kaylah would *die* if she knew her name was in his mouth right now!

'High achiever, that one. So are you. You both went to the circus last year.'

As a reward for those in the top ten percent, we were all given tickets to this B-grade circus that came to town.

The performers were twice as sedated as the animals.

But it was something to do and, at the time, we felt elite.

'I think the school needs to do an audit on its incentives. No wonder we've got kids dropping grades left, right and centre.'

I laugh.

He smiles at my laugh.

'Now, it says here you're on academic watch.'

Dread washes over me.

'You're not getting special considerations.'

I don't really need it.

He squints at his computer.

Rubbing the stubble on his chin.

'In your situation, you should be getting special considerations … Leave it with me.'

He types furiously then stops.

Turns his whole body towards me.

'Now, I'm not going to make you talk, but I just want to say, I know it's not easy. Watching someone you love go through something like that, it's … lonely.'

He drops inside himself like these are more than just words. Something he's felt.

'You're strong. I can see that you're strong.'

SCENE NINE

Home.

I lie on the lounge listening to music when Mum walks in the door, shouldering four shopping bags.

'I thought I told you to put the bins out.'

Hello to you too.

'There are bags of vomit in there'.

Well, that's fucking weird and gross. What happened to a bucket and the toilet?

'Now it's overflowing, and we've got a whole week's worth of rubbish to fit somewhere because we've missed bin day.'

I'm sorry, I forgot.

'How could you forget?'

I love it when she asks questions like that—

Because I have early-onset dementia! How do you think?! I forgot—I didn't remember, that is forgetting.

'I'm not asking for much Sam, I asked you to do one thing.'

She says, dumping the bags on the ground.

I'm fucking sorry, alright.

'DON'T swear at me.'

What's the big deal? Just hide the rubbish in someone else's bin like a normal person.

'It's not the point.'

Why can't you ask Joe?

'Joe has done his chores and this isn't about Joe.'

No. It never is. The fucking golden child.

'ENOUGH! For one second, can you think of someone other than yourself? And for the last time, get your shoes off the lounge.'

She ploughs down the hallway to her bedroom and slams the door.

Her hair looks bad from the back. You can really see her regrowth.

SCENE TEN

Night. Home.

That night, I can't sleep.

Twelve a.m. passes.

Then one a.m.

Now it's two a.m.

Can't lie here anymore.

I go downstairs.

Mum's fallen asleep on the couch with the TV on.

Half a bowl of pasta on the coffee table.

And an empty wine glass on the floor.

She looks smaller than I remember.

There used to be a time when I'd lie in her lap, and she'd play with my hair.

She'd always give the best head rubs.

I don't know when that stopped happening.

But it did.

I turn the TV off and go out the back door.

The beach.

At night, the beach is loud.

I let my ankles sink into the sand.

Imagine myself being pulled under.

A quietness setting in.

Plunging to the bottom of the earth.

I look at my phone.

Kaylah's left me on read.

The voice in my head tells me that things shouldn't be this hard.

I wanna die in a hole in the ground and never wake up.

Turn me into a worm and let me get eaten by a bird.

Not like anyone would notice.

Send.

OH MY GOD?!

Send?!

Fuck.

What have I done?

What the fuck is wrong with me?

Why did I just send that to him??

Now I actually want to end myself.

How the fuck do I retract an email?

I'm going to be sick.

I'm going to be—

It buzzes.

'I would notice.'

What?

I read it five times over.

'I would notice.'

It buzzes again.

'For the record, I think you make a much better person than a worm.'

What is actually happening right now?

I'm so sorry. I didn't mean to send that. It was an accident. It was a joke meant for Kaylah.

Buzz.

'It's okay. Let's chat in the morning. Everything looks better in the morning. Now get some sleep.'

Pause.

And then I feel a tug.

I look up.

The moon.

Glowing.

Just above.

Like I could pluck it out of the sky and stick it in my eye.

This sounds hippy as fuck.

But in this moment, it's like the moon feels me.

And I tug back.

SCENE ELEVEN

School.

I don't know how it happened.

It just became a habit to turn up.

Walk down the corridor.

Past the glass wall of the staff room.

Teachers glancing up over their screens and then back down again.

Like I'm old news.

It's like he's telepathic.

He never seems surprised to see me.

Sometimes I just go there and play on my phone when I can't be bothered to go to class.

Just watch him send emails and make phone calls.

There's a picture I like to look at on his desk.

Of him and a black dog on a farm.

They look so happy.

Where are you?

'At my desk.'

I mean in this photo.

'I know. I'm just teasing. That's my parents' property.'

Is this your dog?

'Yeah.'

What's his name?

'Her name is Bella.'

Bella! That's cute.

He smiles at me and goes back to an email.

I know he likes having me here.

We've become … friends?

He can confide in me.

Which is good.

He tells me how unhappy he is at home.

His wife's a lot of work.

His youngest has autism.

'It's tough for parents who have children with different needs.'

He says, followed by a sigh.

He tells me he reckons half the teachers in this school have autism.

'They're socially fucked, and no-one knows how to wash out a coffee cup.'

He tells me he shouldn't have said that.

But it's no wonder I don't want to go to class.

He tells me the real reason he wears long shirts is because he has a tattoo of green tree python wrapped around his left arm.

No-one knows except me.

He likes my blue hair.

I remind him of a flower.

Which I think is clichéd, but I still feel my cheeks get hot.

He asks me if I can see his greys.

They're just your sparklies.

I tell him.

He likes that.

He says work's stressful but talking to students like me is what keeps him going.

He technically should've reported the emails I sent him.

But knows I didn't mean it.

That everyone overreacts.

'Bureaucracy at its worst.'

He tells me I'm brave.

That there are some people, like Kaylah and Miss Credlin who go through life with no problems.

Those people can never understand.

He grew up with a single mum.

She was hard too.

He can count on one hand the number of times she said 'I love you'.

It feels like nothing exists outside this room.

Like he has nowhere else to be, except here.

Neither do I.

SCENE TWELVE

The beach.

Kaylah and I sit under the only shelter at the beach.

Our usual spot.

Eating chips and drinking slushies.

She asks about Dad.

I don't know what to say, so I just tell her

He's getting there.

'That's good.'

She says, chewing her straw.

I can tell she's glad we're not lingering on the subject.

We're staring at the ocean when I ask—

Do you think you've ever been in love?

'You know I haven't.'

Why haven't we?

'I dunno.'

Is there something wrong with us?

'No.'

Do you think your parents love each other?

'I guess.'

What do you think it's meant to feel like? Love.

Kaylah thinks for a second.

Sucking loudly on her slushy.

Like she's annoyed by the question.

'I think love feels like there are no questions. No other way except them.'

She clutches her head.

'Brain freeze.'

Maybe love feels like brain freeze.

'Painful?'

They say love is messy, right?

Kaylah shakes her head.

'Love shouldn't be messy. Not real love. Real love feels like it should be clean. Like slicing ice. You can see straight through it, but you can also see the edges.'

Edges?

'I don't know. Edges. Where it begins and ends.'

Why would it begin? Why would it end?

'I dunno! It's just something I said. I probably read it in a book.'

She'd live her life in a book if she could.

Speaking of books, can I have your English notes?

She goes quiet.

Kaylah! Your notes? Can I have them?

She carefully puts down her slushy.

'I've been thinking about it … I don't think I should be doing that anymore.'

What?

'I'm happy to proofread your stuff but I can't keep doing the work for you.'

Are you kidding?

'I'm sorry, it's just—we're getting closer to exams.'

Bitch.

I can't believe he was right.

'Who was right?'

No-one. You wouldn't get it.

'O-kay?'

She picks up her slushy.

'I really am sorry.'

Whatever. I've got extra help anyway.

SCENE THIRTEEN

Home.

Glass smashes

Dad collapses on the coffee table.

The sound of sirens

And Mum sobbing

Fill our living room.

I run to let the ambulance officers in

Watch them stab him with adrenalin

It's brutal.

But it works.

An allergic reaction to some new medication, maybe?

They're not sure.

They can't be sure.

So, they wheel him to their van, just to be safe.

It's weird to see a bed outdoors.

I feel like I'm in a gallery looking at an impression of my dad.

A wax dummy, not the real thing.

I run back inside to lock the back door when the ambulance officer points to the floor behind me.

'You're bleeding.'

Shit.

I've trailed blood on the carpet.

Shit!

I was barefoot when I ran to the street.

It's everywhere.

Mum's going to lose it.

I hobble to the kitchen

Frantically searching for the carpet spray under the sink.

By the time I make it back.

The room's empty.

No flashing lights.

No ambulance officers.

The door's open.

Dad's gone.

I thought they were going to wait.

I thought *someone* was going to wait.

A sting.

A piece of glass still stuck in my foot.

I press down.

Leaning into the pain.

It digs in further.

SCENE FOURTEEN

Mr David's office.

It's been two weeks, and it still hurts.

The cut on my foot.

He lets me take off my shoes.

Which helps the pain.

Sorry about my feet. They're gross.

'Nah, you've got cute feet. You should see mine, hairy toes, thick toenails.'

Ewww. Don't tell me you've got a foot fetish or something.

He laughs.

I dunno why I just said that, but he laughed so I feel like it's okay.

'Have you ever had one?'

A foot fetish?

'A boyfriend?'

Oh. Um. No.

He nods.

'Do you want one?'

I can't tell if he's joking.

Not really.

'Why not?'

[Laughs] I dunno. Not interested.

'You're not interested in them, or they're not interested in you?'

Small beat. A change in her.

I dunno.

'So, you're not gay?'

I don't think so.

'Do you think you're pretty?'

Not really.

'Why did you dye your hair that colour?'

Dunno.

'Don't get me wrong, I love it, I love that you stand out. You don't have to be classically beautiful like Lizzie Thomas. Or athletic like Cecilia Patsan.'

I get pins and needles in the back of my neck.

'You're different from the other girls in your year.'

He inches closer.

'You're real.'

I don't move.

'You're the kind of girl I'd want my son to date.'

I stop breathing.

'The kind of girl I would've dreamed of dating in high school.'

He leans in.

'Relax. You don't need to hide from me.'

His lips touch mine.

They're wet.

I wish I was wearing my shoes.

SCENE FIFTEEN

School.

Don't know how long it's been but I still haven't gone to his office.

I see him walking around on lunch duty.

In his high-vis vest.

Like we can't see him without it.

He goes up to the music kids, takes their guitar.

Strums once.

They're so giddy.

They're basically giving him a standing ovation.

Admittedly, these are the instruments he helped get donated.

They've *got* to be grateful.

He bows.

They laugh and clap.

I hate him.

I watch him compliment Lucy on her fingernails.

She dangles them in front of him.

Flirting with her fingertips.

She wishes.

Lucy used to have cold showers because she heard it helped you lose weight.

Gave herself four UTIs in the process.

He looks directly at me while talking to Mrs Shelton.

Keeping eye contact while simultaneously ignoring me.

She's blushing. Twisting her wedding ring like it's tempting.

I hate him.

I avoid him for as long as I can, but he catches me off guard.

'Sam. Can I speak to you for a second?'

The yoyo in my stomach drops. I want to run but it's like there's concrete in my shoes.

'I think we need to talk about what happened the other week. You can't keep avoiding me.'

I chew the inside of my cheek.

'I think we both know what happened was a mistake.'

Understatement of the century.

'I think we both know that. And I hope that we can move forward from this. Not let it tarnish a good thing.'

Okay?

'Perhaps an apology is in order. That way we can forgive and forget?'

Yes. God. Please. Anything for this to be over.

'You don't have to do it now; you can take your time if you want.'

[Confused] *What?*

'It's flattering. Really. And you're not the first.'

I don't ... understand ...

'I know you didn't mean it. It's just a crush.'

My heart stops beating.

'But I still think, for good measure, you should apologise.'

Me.

[Stuttering] I—I—

I'm sorry.

Beat.

He nods his head like he got what he wanted.

'Don't look so worried. I said forgive and forget.'

I can't explain why.

But I smile.

And say—thank you.

Because what else am I going to do?

SCENE SIXTEEN

The library.

I sit

Barely lucid

In Kaylah's study group.

The only way I can see her.

Half listening to a group of girls who all wear glasses talk about hidden quadratics or some shit.

When Lucy says,

'Oh my god, did you hear? Jasmin's officially lost it.'

They all smirk.

'What's she done now?'

'She's gone too far this time. She reckons a teacher tried to stick his hand up her skirt. Grabbed her on the ass.'

What?

'I know, it's fucked up.'

Which teacher?

'Dunno.'

'We all know she's just jaded because her twenty-five-year-old mechanic boyfriend broke up with her.'

'It's kind of embarrassing now.'

'Why is she even here? Like just drop out and become a hairdresser already.'

'She can't just say that and get away with it.'

'Like, there are actual consequences.'

Maybe it's true?

Small beat.

They all look at me like I'm crazy.

'No offence but who'd risk their career for Jasmin?'

'Yeah, she's probably riddled with STIs.'

'Let's be honest, that's the real risk.'

They all laugh.

Including Kaylah.

SCENE SEVENTEEN

School, again.

I'm banging the vending machine.

Willing a Sprite to come loose

When I hear the clicking of heels behind me.

'Sam?'

I see Miss Credlin's reflection looking at me.

I squish my forehead into the glass. It's cold.

'Shouldn't you be in class?'

SAM *turns lethargically.*

I have a free period.

She purses her lips like she doesn't believe me.

'Free periods are meant for study and revision.'

I'm doing the Pomodoro Technique; this is my five-minute break.

'Well, in that case, come on.'

What?

'My next student isn't for another forty-five minutes. I want to catch up on your break.'

I don't move.

'Otherwise, I'll have to report that you're out of class.'

SAM *sighs.*

School counsellor's office.

The chair is itchy.

I can't stop rattling my foot and picking at my nails.

She notices.

Gives me a squishy ball to squeeze.

I hate that it actually helps.

'Talking to me is not meant to be a punishment. Some people even find it enjoyable.'

She tries to brush an ant off her desk.

There's a line of them crawling up the wall.

She catches me looking.

'I've tried to get rid of them. But they just keep coming back.'

Maybe they'd go away if you stopped eating at your desk.

Oh shit.

I said that out loud.

Sorry, I didn't—(mean)

'No. You're right. It's a bad habit. Sometimes I think there just isn't enough time in the day for lunch.'

She looks embarrassed.

Takes off her glasses and looks through them. They're covered in smudges and fingerprints and the frame is slightly bent.

I think about her terrible salary.

The piles of paperwork on her desk.

Her computer, covered in sticky notes.

'It's good to see you again.'

She feels different.

Older. Softer.

Or maybe she's just tired.

'What's new?'

The question echoes in my ears.

She holds my gaze like she actually wants to know.

I wish she could read my mind.

So, I didn't have to say it.

I could tell her

If I could just …

Start.

If I could just

Find the words

The *right* words

To start

To say it.

Out loud.

I can do it.

I'm going to do it

I'm going to open my mouth and …

'Knock knock.'

We look up.

[*Mr David*] *'I thought I saw Sam come in here.'*

[*Miss Credlin*] *'Yes, we're just checking in.'*

[*Mr David*] *'Gosh, you do wonders for this school Miss Credlin, I don't know where we'd be without you.'*

So much for a wet blanket.

[*Mr David*] *'Just wanted to know if you were putting in for Lara's going-away present?'*

[*Miss Credlin*]. *'Oh. I thought I replied to the email. Sorry. Yes, count me in.'*

[*Mr David*] *'Excellent. And apologies I won't be able to make this afternoon's meeting. We're holding a family funeral for Bella.'*

[*Miss Credlin*] *'Oh no, I'm so sorry to hear.'*

[*Mr David*] *'It was her own fault really. She was chasing a rabbit and her leg got caught in the fence. Mangled herself up.'*

[*Miss Credlin*] *'Oh gosh.'*

[*Mr David*] *'Had to put her down myself. It's kinder that way.'*

He looks at me as he says it.

[**Mr David**] *'Anyway, I'll count you in for the gift. Good to see you, Sam. For a second I thought you were avoiding me, but we still need to talk about your plan for next year. Don't let me interrupt. Enjoy the girl chat.'*

SCENE EIGHTEEN

School.

Blood trickles down my leg.

Kaylah grabs at my arm.

'Stop! I thought you said you weren't doing that anymore!'

I'm not.

'So, what's that?'

Pointing to the cut on my thigh.

I just wasn't paying attention.

'That looks deep.'

It's FINE.

'Give it here.'

No.

'What were you doing it with? Scissors?'

Relax. It was just the lid of my pen.

'Sharp fucking lid.'

She tries to march me to the bathroom.

Let go!

'No.'

Fucking let go!

She does.

Shaking her head at me.

Why are you shaking your head?

'Why do you think? You've just fucked up your leg.'

You're so annoying.

'What's going on with you?'

What's going on with me? Hmm, I wonder what's going on with me. Not much, oh, except for the fact that my dad is basically a peanut, my mum's a wafer cracker and my brother's a cunt. But other than that, it's hard to know.

'Sam. This is not okay.'

Oh my god. Would you stop overreacting!

'Don't you care?'

About what?

'Yourself?!'

Why should I? It's not like anyone else gives a shit.

'God, you're so self-centred sometimes!'

What the fuck?

'I know it sounds harsh, but you can't keep doing this.'

You don't get it. How could you? Miss Perfect. You don't actually care about me.

'Yes, I do!'

I'm just someone to have around to make your life seem better.

'What are you talking about?!'

Let's be honest, after school, I'd give us a year, tops. Maybe it's best we part ways now.

And then she starts.

Are you serious? What the fuck are you crying about?

Beat.

'You. Sam. You need help.'

SCENE NINETEEN

I sit in the girls' toilets for hours.

Watching and rewatching the video of Jasmin.

I watch him scoop her up.

His hands grabbing her flesh.

Lingering dangerously close to her skirt.

I want to scream at him to *get away from her!*

To stop touching her!

She looks small.

Wriggling like a child.

The laptop.

Why was she smashing it?

What did he do?

I watch it again and again and again.

Until I'm out the front of the staff room.

In front of the door.

Ready to unleash

To fight back.

When I hear it

His voice.

In the corridor

In my head?

Rattling through my bones.

Getting louder and louder.

I try to hold on

But the courage.

It's gone.

SCENE TWENTY

On my way home.

It pours with rain.

My socks are soaking wet.

Hair sticks to my face.

I can feel myself getting tinier with every step I take.

There's no point running.

If you run,

You run into the rain.

It's better to just—

Let it hit you.

A lady struts past holding her umbrella.

Smug bitch.

Well, I'm fine.

I'm not cold.

I'm shaking but I'm not cold.

Fuck.

I'm shaking so much

It's like

I could crack open the footpath.

Make cars crash into telegraph poles.

Shake the houses

Until bookcases topple over

And all the porcelain in the world is just dust on the floor.

And everything fragile is broken.

And people have no choice

But to run onto the street to see

What's going on.

Of course, no-one does.

Why would they?

A car with aggressive windscreen wipers flashes its lights at me.

I ignore it.

It slows down next to me.

It beeps.

The window winds down.

'Get in.'

I want to say no.

'You can't walk home in this. Get in.'

I hate myself

Because I do.

I get in.

Kaylah was right.

SCENE TWENTY-TWO

Home.

The front door is wide open.

Music blasts from the living room.

Mum swoops me into her arms.

She's grinning.

She's wearing lipstick and grinning.

Joe's even here. Wearing a button-up shirt.

I can't tell if I'm hallucinating.

Or if I'm dead.

[**Mum**] *'Honey, you're saturated. Don't tell me you walked home in this? You should've called! We would've picked you up.'*

[**Joe**] *'Don't you have an umbrella?'*

[**Mum**] *'Here.'*

Mum hands me a tea towel and a glass of champagne.

What's going on?

[**Mum**] *'Your dad got the all-clear.'*

What?

[**Mum**] *'Cheers everyone!'*

I look over at Dad. He raises his glass in my direction.

[**Dad**] *'We did it, kiddo! We bloody did it.'*

Then sculls his champagne in one.

[**Mum**] *'Quick! Get changed. We're going out for dinner! Joe, book us an Uber!'*

I look back to Dad, he's dancing.

[**Dad**] *'No more bad news for the rest of the year!'*

Without moving.

I start crying.

[**Mum**] *'Oh. Come here darling, you beautiful girl.'*

Mum pulls me into her chest and kisses my head.

I can smell her perfume.

Dad piles on.

Even Joe joins in.

Wrapping his arms around.

We stand there.

A clump of a family.

Holding each other.

I don't think I've ever clung to anything so tightly.

SCENE TWENTY-THREE

The fish and chip shop.

Joe and I lean up against the wall, waiting for our order.

I try to trick myself into thinking everything's back to normal.

The chip lady is as slow as ever.

Wiping the sweat off her forehead with the back of her freckly hand.

Probably works the hardest. Gets paid the least.

It stinks in here.

Reeks.

She's probably gotten used to it.

The smell.

Or doesn't know any different.

And then I see it.

In the gap between the drink fridge and the counter

Its long wiry tail curled at the end.

The rat.

Daring me to look away.

Daring me to unsee it.

But I see it.

I can't unsee it.

It's fucking disgusting.

SCENE TWENTY-FOUR

Supermarket car park.

All I know is that she works at the supermarket.

I ask around

Until I find her in the underground car park sitting in a trolley picking at a scab on her knee.

I storm straight up to her—

Jasmin?

Without moving.

'Wut?'

She's not super friendly.

I didn't actually pre-plan this.

I don't know if you know me, but we go to school together.

She looks up through her thick mascara.

'Yeah, blue hair. I've seen you.'

Well, I know this might be weird because we've never really talked before but—

'I don't have any.'

Sorry?

'I already told the others. I won't have my supply till Tuesday.'

Supply?

'Ritalin. Dexies … ?'

Oh. No. That's not why I'm here.

'What do you want then? Can't you see I'm working?'

Yeah, of course. Um. I just wanted to say that I heard what happened to you.

She rolls her eyes and goes back to picking at the scab.

And I want you to know I believe you … About Mr David.

She stops picking.

Is that who it was?

'I dunno what you're talking about.'

Did he do that?

SAM *points.*

Jasmin quickly cups her neck to hide the hickeys.

'What the fuck is your problem?'

I think you should tell someone. I can come with you.

'Who the fuck are you?'

If you don't say something, he could do it to other people.

'I fuckin' did. And you know what I got? Fuckin' nothing.'

I mean a teacher or the police.

'Why the fuck do you care, anyway?'

She jumps out of the trolley and shoves me in the chest.

'Huh?'

I just want to help you.

'Get the fuck away from me.'

Please, Jasmin—

'You've got five seconds to fuck off or I'm gunna beat the shit out of you.'

I just thought—

'Five'

If you needed help to—

'Four'

Do it, I could—

'Three'

I want to keep pleading but I don't.

I back away.

Leave her alone.

I don't know what I expected

If I can't do it

Why would she?

SCENE TWENTY-FIVE

School.

I don't know what day it is

Every day is a fog

I feel like I'm made from wax

No.

Honeycomb

My insides are honeycomb

Hollow

Spent.

I walk down the steps

Through the noise of it all.

On my way to skip school for the twentieth time this week.

Past the music rooms

Through the girls in lemon yellow

And the boys in baby blue.

Past the C-Block toilets

Past the canteen

The library

The teachers, congregating.

Wonder if I'll make it through the day

And then I see Liam *reach* for Kaylah's bra

Grabbing it around the strap

He pulls it like a slingshot and lets it slap against her back.

She goes to scream

But doesn't.

Just steels herself with a silent strength she shouldn't have to have.

And then he says it.

'Fucking frigid.'

I see it

In her eyes.

In her jaw.

Her pain

Her fight.

My friend.

And something inside me punctures

Ruptures.

Hot pumping furious love for her.

HOW DARE HE?!

My legs jolt.

Towards him

HOW DARE YOU TOUCH HER!

I hurl his backpack across the gravel.

He flinches.

And I am taken.

Fist to wood.

I bang

And I bang

And I bang

And I bang

She opens the door

A cup of tea steaming in her hand.

'Sam?'

My heart opens.

Finally

I let it all out.

SCENE TWENTY-SIX

I count six.

Police officers.

As they walk down the hallways past the plaques on the walls.

Towards his office.

Teachers glance up over their computer screens and then quickly back down again.

Like it's old news.

Like it has nothing to do with them.

I watch him surrendering his hands to the air.

Palms to the sky.

Looking up and seeing me.

Towering over him.

He cries onto his business shirt.

Like a wounded child.

All eyes on him.

As he is walked down the stairs.

Headfirst into the backseat of the car.

Pleading.

Begging.

Not to do this.

Beat.

It didn't happen like that.

I don't know how it happened.

I wasn't at school that day.

I assume it was quick.

Quiet.

I know what people will say.

I can already hear the murmurs.

I tell myself

I don't care.

I know what happened.

Kaylah and I sit on the beach.

Not under the shelter.

We tried.

But it was riddled with five-year-olds in party hats.

Happy birthday, Johnny.

Instead, we sit in the sand.

It's warm.

We don't talk.

Just watch.

As the waves go in and out.

The tide seems far away.

Without looking.

She holds my hand.

Her skin is soft.

She squeezes me.

And I squeeze her back.

END